WARMTH

WHY WE STAY WARM TO REFUEL

by Harriet Brundle

BEARPORT
PUBLISHING

Minneapolis, Minnesota

FUEL Up!

Credits:

Cover & Throughout - Rhenzy, notkoo, zsooofija, Kastoluza, Svitlana Bezuhlova, TravnikovStudio, Olya_Beli_Art, 4&5 - Rvector, supot phanna, Tartila, 6&7 - Rawpixel.com,   Zhenyakot, Nina Puankova, 8&9 - NotionPic, Rawpixel.com, 10&11 - MANDY GODBEHEAR, Kastoluza, katarina_1, 12&13 - fotogestoeber, Kakigori Studio, Mister_X, 14&15 - ann131313, Suiraton, Brian A Jackson, 16&17 - vystekimages, 18&19 - ann131313, Robert Kneschke, 20&21 - Olesya Kuznetsova, Kenishirotie, 22&23 - graphego, vectoratu, Suiraton, Focus_Vector, curiosity, ITisha.

Images are courtesy of Shutterstock.com. With thanks to Getty Images, Thinkstock Photo, and iStockphoto.

Library of Congress Cataloging-in-Publication Data

Names: Brundle, Harriet, author.
Title: Warmth : why we stay warm to refuel / by Harriet Brundle.
Description: Fusion. | Minneapolis, MN : Bearport Publishing Company, 2021] | Series: Fuel up! | Includes bibliographical references and index.
Identifiers: LCCN 2020009348 (print) | LCCN 2020009349 (ebook) | ISBN 9781647473457 (library binding) | ISBN 9781647473501 (paperback) | ISBN 9781647473556 (ebook)
Subjects: LCSH: Body temperature—Regulation—Juvenile literature. | Adaptation (Physiology)—Juvenile literature.
Classification: LCC QP135 .B78 2021 (print) | LCC QP135 (ebook) | DDC 612/.01426—dc23
LC record available at https://lccn.loc.gov/2020009348
LC ebook record available at https://lccn.loc.gov/2020009349

For more information, write to Bearport Publishing, 5357 Penn Avenue South, Minneapolis, MN 55419. Printed in the United States of America.

CONTENTS

ALL ABOUT WARMTH

To be healthy, our bodies must stay at the right **temperature**. We can learn how warm we are by using a thermometer.

THERMOMETERS

BEING AT THE RIGHT TEMPERATURE HELPS OUR BODIES STAY FUELED UP!

Not everyone's body is the same. Body temperature can be different based on our age, our **sex**, or even the time of day.

MY BODY TEMPERATURE

If your body is over 100.4 degrees Fahrenheit (38 degrees Celcius) or under 95°F (35°C), it might be a problem. If you are too hot or too cold, you should see a doctor.

If you've been exercising or if it's a hot day, your body might be warmer. If it's a cold day, your body might be cooler.

GETTING TOO HOT

If you get too hot, you might start to sweat. Sweat is mostly made of water. The sweat on our skin **evaporates**, cooling us down.

If you're sick, your body might become hotter. A high temperature can mean that you have a **fever**.

IF YOU FEEL SICK, TELL AN ADULT RIGHT AWAY.

9

GETTING TOO COLD

If you feel cold, it means that your body temperature has become lower. When you are chilly, your teeth might chatter and your skin might feel cold.

If you are feeling very cold, heat yourself up by putting on warm clothes and moving your body around.

IF YOU STILL FEEL COLD, MAKE SURE YOU TELL AN ADULT.

SHIVERING

Our bodies have different ways to keep us at the right temperature. When we get cold, we shiver.

When we shiver, our **muscles** move very quickly. We shake. By doing this, our muscles make heat, which warms us up.

MUSCLE

HYPOTHERMIA

Hypothermia happens when a person's body temperature is below 95°F (35°C). They may shiver, feel confused, or breathe very quickly.

If someone has hypothermia, call 911. Try to make sure the person goes indoors, gets into dry clothes, and is wrapped in a blanket.

STAYING THE RIGHT TEMPERATURE

If you're feeling warm, try to drink plenty of water and wear loose, light clothes. Try to stay out of the sun if it's hot outside.

If you're feeling too cold, put on some extra clothing, like a sweater, hat, and gloves. When it's cold outside, try to stay indoors and have warm drinks.

17

OUR SMART BODIES

Our brains help make sure that our bodies stay warm enough but not too warm.

BRAIN

The steps our brains take to cool us down or warm us up happen without us having to think about it.

A HEALTHY LIFESTYLE

To keep our bodies the right temperature, it's important to eat well. We need foods from different groups.

CARBS

DAIRY

PROTEIN

FRUITS AND VEGETABLES

Exercise is a great way to stay healthy, but make sure that you don't overheat. Sleeping well will also help keep you fueled up.

Fuel Up with Warmth!

Try to match how you should dress with each of these types of weather. Which clothes are best on a hot, snowy, or rainy day?

How warm are you? Place a thermometer under your armpit. Keep your arm close to your body for a few minutes. When you check the thermometer, it should show your temperature.

WHAT IS YOUR TEMPERATURE?

GLOSSARY

evaporates turns from a liquid into a gas or vapor, usually through heat

fever when the body temperature is much higher than normal, often causing shivering and a headache

fueled when there is enough energy or power to do something

hypothermia a condition where the body temperature is lower than normal

light thin and not weighing very much

muscles the parts of the body that move the body around

sex being male or female

temperature how hot or cold something is

INDEX